The Weenie Book

By D.T. Carter

FREE Bonuses: "The Weenie Book" Audiobook and Action/Discussion Guide
+ The Weenie Book Poster

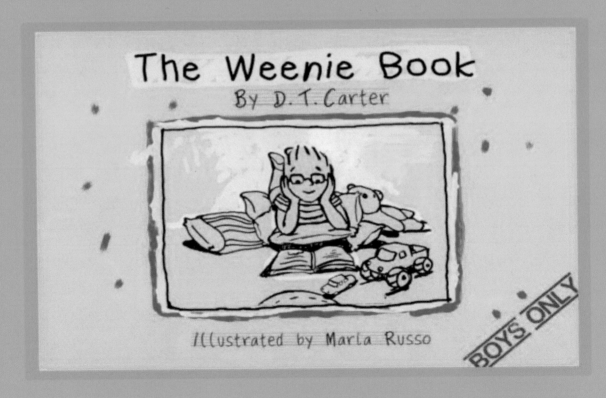

You can now listen to the "The Weenie Book" at home or on the run with your son. It is full of sound effects and comes with the theme song for "The Weenie Book".

Also, you'll be able to download the Action/Discussion Guide that will help you talk with your son about the different topics discussed in "The Weenie Book".

Finally, when you download The Pee Pee Guide Poster you will have a fun guide to teach your son about getting his pee in the toilet.

Please visit:
www.donaldtcarter.com/free-wb
To download your AWESOME FREEBIES

Dear Parents,

We are living in difficult times, aren't we? What society once deemed as "bad" is now "good", and what was once known as "good" is now "bad", according to the same society.

My intent in writing this book is to use the vocabulary of a young boy. It should be used as a tool to help you talk to your child (3-6 year old boy) about his penis. This content should not be seen as offensive, but as a light-hearted way to help you promote a healthy sexuality in your child according to our Creator's plan.

Later books in this "Weenie Book" series will promote proper etiquette in the bathroom as well as what it means to have a penis.

It is my prayer that you (Mom, Dad or Guardian) will use this book to talk to your son about how to care for his penis and teach him more about how to behave with it.

May God bless you as you work hard to raise your boy!

D.T. Carter

Original title: The Weenie Book
Self Published by: Donald Thomas Carter
Contact: dt@donaldtcarter.com

Illustration and design: Maria Russo

Hi! I'm Gabe! I have a penis like all boys do.

I like to call it "weenie" because it reminds me of a hot dog. Hehe!

One day at preschool I had my hand on my weenie during story time. My teacher Mrs. Stevenson yelled at me, "Gabriel Green, you stop that right now!"

I don't know why she got so mad, but I felt really bad about touching my weenie.

When I'm sad, my Daddy always makes me feel better. So, I told him all about what happened when I got home from school.

He said, "Gabe, touching your weenie isn't wrong, but there is a time and place to do it."

"And school isn't the time or place."

I think my daddy is really cool. I like to hang out with him and watch cartoons.

He has a weenie too, so sometimes, I like to talk to him about my weenie.

He tells, "God gave you a weenie and that's NOT a bad thing. It's AWESOME to have one, Gabe!"

I like my weenie, and I think he's right.

Almost every day, he teaches me something new about having a weenie.

He says, "Wash it really good when you take a bath."

"If you don't, it will stink and might hurt when you pee, and then I would have to take you to the doctor."

Sometimes I like to play with my weenie.

The other day, I was taking a bath, and daddy saw me stick it in an empty shampoo bottle.

No! Don't do that!" he said, as he laughed out loud.

"It can get stuck and I would have to call the fire department to get it out!"

Mommy doesn't like to know about me playing with it, but daddy says it is fine.

He says, "You can play with your weenie, but there is a time and place to do it."

He also tells me to NEVER EVER play with it when others are around.

"It can make them feel weird and never want to come back to our house."

Sometimes I like to stretch my weenie. Daddy asks me, "Are you playing go-go-gadget weenie?" and that makes me laugh.

"Don't stretch it too far or it might fall off," he tells me.

I don't think that can happen, but it does hurt when I pull it too far.

Sometimes I like to rub my weenie on things when I have my clothes on.

Daddy says, "It's OK, but don't rub it raw, "cause it might hurt when you pee."

I don't know what 'rub it raw' means, but I don't want it to hurt when I pee.

Sometimes, when I touch it, rub it, stretch it, or play with it, or for no reason at all, it gets bigger and harder.

Daddy says, "Don't worry Gabe! God made it that way and it happens to all boys."

But...

"Never, ever show or tell anyone that your weenie is bigger.

No one should know about that, or see that your weenie is bigger," he tells me.

Daddy and mommy always tell me the most important thing is, "NEVER, EVER show it to anyone or let anyone touch it whether it is big or small."

And, "NEVER, EVER let anyone show their weenie to you, or touch anyone's weenie, whether they are a big person or a kid just like you.

Also, if anyone does any of these things or makes me fell weird with their weenie, I need to tell my parents or another adult I trust right away and I won't be in trouble."

Sometimes the boys at preschool think it's funny to show off their weenies in the bathroom.

That's when I remember what mommy and daddy always say...

I tell the boys, "NO! your private parts are private! Don't show them to anyone!" Then I tell Mrs. Stevenson.

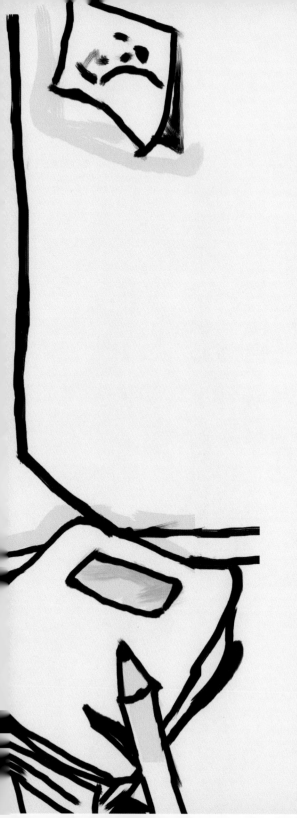

I used to think that having a weenie was a bad thing, because of the time Mrs. Stevenson yelled at me, and when grandma made a face after I told her it was bigger.

But now I know that having a weenie is not a bad thing at all.

I just need to remember that I have to wash it really well and never show it to anyone or let anyone touch it.

Also, that there is a time and place to touch it, stretch it, rub it, and play with it.

That time and place is when I'm alone at home in my bedroom.

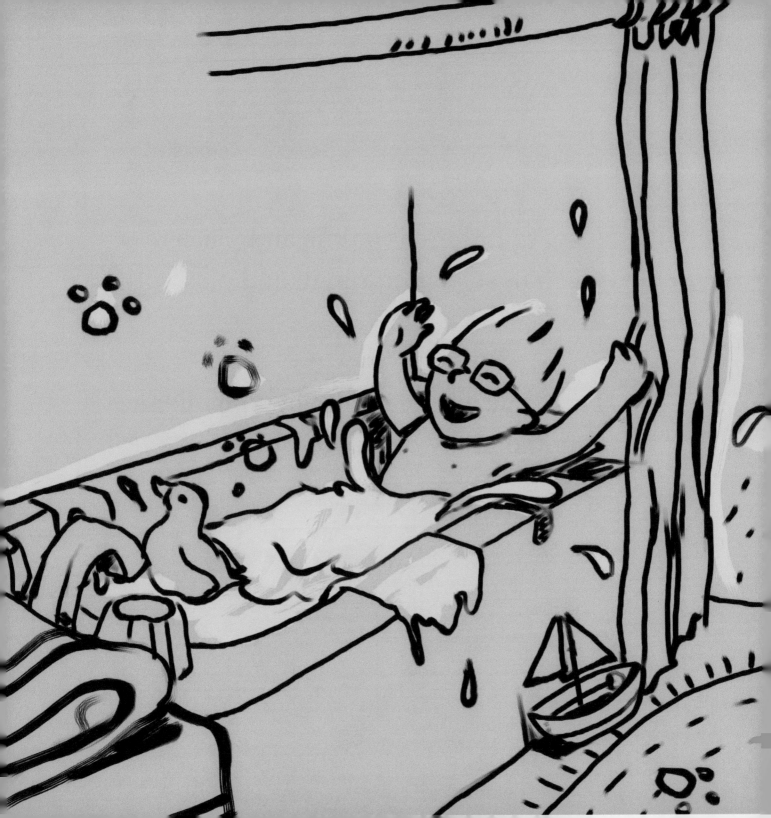

And as Daddy always tell me...

"Whether it is big or small, my weenie is a present to me from God, and I need to take care of it and protect it."

Having a weenie is awesome!

I'm so happy that God made me a boy and gave me a weenie!

Buy The Other Books in The Weenie Book Series!

Find the 4 books here:
www.donaldtcarter/weenie-book-series

Printed in Great Britain
by Amazon

28891175R00027